Fall Is Here!

By Jane Belk Moncure

Illustrated by Frances Hook

THE CHILD'S WORLD
ELGIN, ILLINOIS 60120

Library of Congress Cataloging in Publication Data

Moncure, Jane Belk.
  Fall Is Here!

  SUMMARY: Describes in verse the various activities
and changes associated with the fall.
  [1. Fall—Fiction. 2. Stories in rhyme] I. Hook,
Frances. II. Title.
PZ8.3.M72Fal   [E]   75-14019
ISBN 0-913778-13-3

PICTURE WORDS

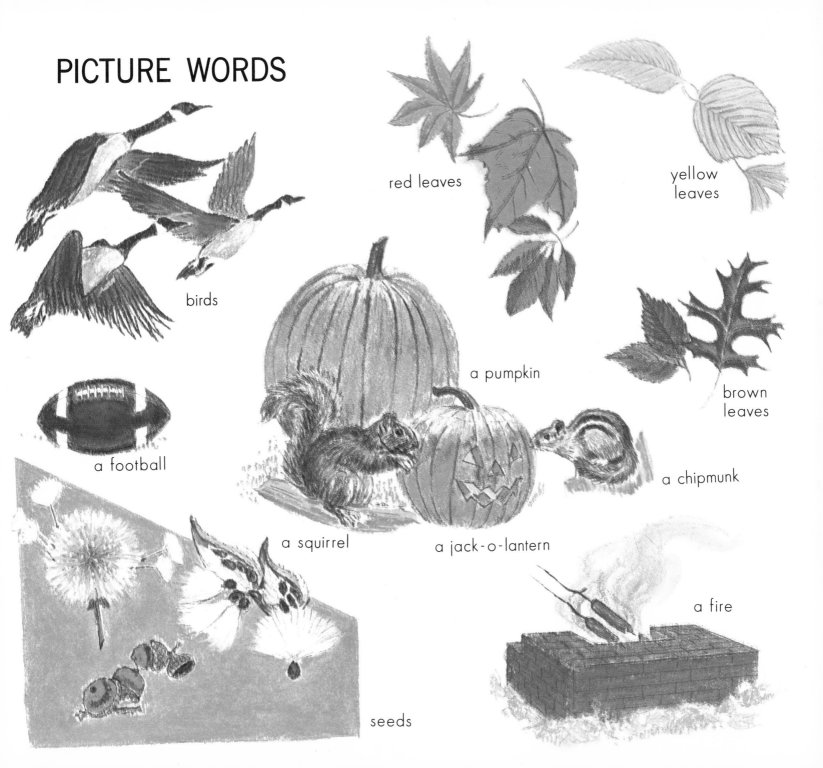

birds

red leaves

yellow leaves

a pumpkin

brown leaves

a football

a squirrel

a jack-o-lantern

a chipmunk

seeds

a fire

I like fall.

Do you like fall?

I like football best of all.

I like fall.

Leaves fall down, like raindrops,
yellow, red, and brown.

I can be a leaf. I turn around.

Guess what happens? I fall down!

Where do birds fly on a fall day?

I hear them cry, "Goodby, goodby."

Why do some birds fly away?

I do not know where some birds go.

I know where I go on a fall day.

I go to the park and stay after dark.

Fall is the nicest time of all
to buy a pumpkin.
Do you know why?
It is time for a jack-o-lantern
and a pumpkin pie.

Do you like fall
     when cold winds blow,
      up above and down below?

I can be the wind.
Seeds blow away.
Where do seeds go
     on a cold fall day?

Up

and

down

and

around

they

go!

Will a little squirrel find them?

Do
you
know?

Where do leaves go when fall winds blow?

Up

and

down

and around

they

go.

Where do little chipmunks go?

Do you know?

In fall a fire feels warm and bright.
Will fires burn on a winter night?

Will my jack-o-lantern glow
when winter comes with ice and snow?

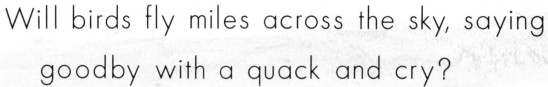

Will birds fly miles across the sky, saying goodby with a quack and cry?

I play football every day in fall. Can you guess what I will play on a snowy winter day?

Autumn Leaves